FIRE DINER
poems and shorts

by Zack Kopp

ISBN 13: 978-0615778228

Published by Magic Trash Press

PRINTED IN THE UNITED STATES OF AMERIC

for all the mothers and the fathers

TABLE OF CONTENTS

WARNING 1

THE STARS 2

THE OPERATION 3

PREGNANT PAUSE 4

THE RELATIVES 5

SCIENCE FICTION 7

MEMORIAL DAY 8

THE SHY PRIVATE EYE 10

SOMETIMES CELEBRITIES 13

WAY DOWN 14

SHADOW VALLEY 16

CRAZY JOHNNY YUMA 17

MY POLITICS 18

LISTEN 19

ALBUQUERQUE 20

STATIC 21

SHARP AND SWEET 24

RTD JOURNALS #7 25

REMEMBER 28

PLANET LADY 29

THOUSANDS OF YEARS 20

CHILDHOOD 32

THE TOTAL WORK OF ART 33

WHERE GREASY DUCKTAILS ARE SMOOTHED INTO PLACE 34

THE SNAKE OIL ADDICT 36

AND THE YELLOW LAND YAWNED 40

GENERATION X THINKS ABOUT SOAP OPERAS 43

THE DEVIL'S BARN 44

POTS AND PANS 46

SOMETIMES IT'S A JOYRIDE 48

THE WATER PARTY 49

IN TEXAS 51

THE THIEF 52

WILLPOWER 53

FAME 55

FROM A SPEEDING CAR 57

THE SUN 59

WESTERNERS 60

A MORNING SHOW BANNED IN THE WEST AND MADE INTO A LATE-LATE 63

THE SECRET AGENTS 65

DAYLIGHT 66

UNFORGOTTEN 67

THE SMELL OF LIMES 68

PURGATORY 69

THE PULL OF THE DROP 70

THE STUPID LONESOME 72

MODERN ART 73

IN KANSAS 75

COUNTRY LIVING 76

"NOW LET'S HAVE A PICNIC!" 77

ARMCHAIR FRABNKENSTEINS 79

THE SARCASTIC INDIAN 80

RTD JOURNALS #17 81

THE WONDERFUL JACKET 82

OUTSIDER ART 84

MEANING 86

WARNING

Without this information you will die in a world you never understood and be reborn in another still more puzzling. It will happen again and again. You will never again be as close to the truth as you are at this moment.

THE STARS

The cold stars clicking their claws together like crabs in a tank. History changes and runs off the page like butter. The world has been dragged through me, and I've been dragged through the world. We're even. Stars twirl over stinking trenches, beginning a subtle magnetic resurrection that will take all time and never end. The mind is a machine to move matter. The scenes are super modern. The earth has us, and we multiply. Founded in an impulse of wild lonely need, not serious planning. The stars dissolve in my mouth not my hand. Let this life not be a torment. Let the stars stop shaking. I will turn my greatest tricks for you.

THE OPERATION

This guy I knew worked there

he had all his ideas pulled out with pliers

It came out through his nose   every thought he'd ever had.

Each time a new one landed in the pan

the company's computers picked it up and translated it to video

then broadcast it on a screen above the stretcher for the others to watch while they worked

His mind had thoughts about the ocean, death, the moon, women's eyes and hearts and tits and cunts, all the times he'd gone down on his knees in the mud for the truth, crosseyed and singsonging, all the promises he'd made to others

all still there

Years and years of bewildered energy oozing out slowly in a broad greasy slick like blood or honey or oil slipping down his cheek into the drain and collecting in the stainless-steel pan underneath the stretcher

Outside idiot nature kept waiting

"The joy of waiting! The joy of waiting!" it sang.

PREGNANT PAUSE

All the lean years living on the lining of the planet as the dying sun dwindles, cars cough in the street like sick cows and green smells float from the sofa.

Kids with grins like the grills of trucks throw dogshit at the soldiers and rubble smoulders where temples and palaces were. Girls with gills like fish and eels in dresses made of sack give dirt-cheap head beneath a ruined staircase. The kids light cigarettes with burning rocks and men with hearts like bombs work plots in the darkness, hunched over maps with flashlights.

It has taken a thousand years. Official policy is not to shoot the kids but sometimes a soldier loses his temper.

Two rivers flow through the land and the sun is a searing hole.

The people wear white and swaddle their heads in respect.

Men in hoods with hearts like bombs are filing their teeth in the darkness. Cockroaches nestle in cracks in the walls, clicking their feelers together and glistening horribly.

An old man pushes the ghost of his son past the shops and bars in an empty wheelchair.

THE RELATIVES

It was hard to relate

I kept trying to make them all come back alive

but I couldn't think of anything to say

that would make life seem better than death

except that life kept letting you think you had

another chance   until they all ran out

but that was really kind of a dirty trick

on life's part you know

so I didn't say it

I kept on talking just in case

"I mean, being dead is easier, I guess . . .

just not as exciting. And it's bigger in a

way too, it doesn't come with walls around it

like being alive does, I mean there isn't any time, so

everything happens at once, and you don't get so *worried*

from moment to moment, you know . . ."

I wanted them to know I really cared

I was on their side, and I tried to let them know

I kept moving among them I tried to relate

I got very impassioned

I started to feel like Kenneth Patchen

"Alright, never mind."

SCIENCE FICTION

He lived alone and never wrote science fiction. For many years sealed away in an old hotel room with only one window and a greasy yellow plastic shade you pull down by hand. The exact location of this was never known, but it changes and spreads underneath us. Like a clipping under smeary plastic in a family album. The wind playing break-up music in the trees outside. After bringing things right to the edge and letting them go. He may be down there right now hammering away at his next masterpiece, pulling up stars by the roots and flinging them down into an old frying pan to spit fat and sizzle. That's where the stars ended up in his stories. His fiction was a streamlined dream animal, the typewriter cackled in the night like a Gatling gun, and jumped around on the table when he hit the keys. A symphony in a tin can.

MEMORIAL DAY

outside people are slamming the lids of

dumpsters   I think   or unloading a big

clanging metal object in the alley

obtrusive   loud   I don't know why

it's Tuesday night   sometimes I hear

lots of explosions outside

a made wave in the air

that moves   but I can't tell whether it's

thunder or fireworks

I think it's fireworks

that's how it sounds

excited and fast   like firecrackers

is this a holiday?

I sit here listening   watching TV

FIRE DINER

on the banks of a giant strange world

at the very edge

whirlybirds chopping the air overhead

my life is always in the balance

THE SHY PRIVATE EYE

My head's a rotten apple

Time is a tiny flame beneath my heels that nips and bites

Something good will happen soon

So what if the world is mashed and muddled with beauty and ugliness, horror and mercy, shit and light, the one springing up from a patch of the other—so what if the world's a maze, and the wondering soul gets lost if it wanders?

Time goes on, and life goes on, and we all get kicked in the head again and again so we know there's a wall

and we keep on trying

My years as a private eye have left me oddly stunned and shy

I walk past houses now, kids screaming inside

Kids screaming

all the time, sure, but who knows, right?

And I keep on walking

 You see how it is

I'm shy

this secret agent needs a spine.

FIRE DINER

And cuckoo-clocks

Ever since the Birthday Bomber case

Kids and clocks

I'm not afraid of the bats and demons

Time rolls on razor wheels or crawls with suckers

Time flutters behind us at every scene

You walk under trees

and the leaves shake the drops down over you, some cloud's

helpless piss all over your hat like a practical joke

Warm in here but my soul feels funny. My head feels soft.

My life is full of pain and through all the pain I can dimly remember

a time when my life was not full of pain

As a private detective

I have begun to detect a delicious soreness in all my limbs

that lets me know the spring is here

Let it ring from the ashy places, the dripping gutters full of spiders.

Let the rain fill my boots as I walk

A light is on

A hundred lights are on

SOMETIMES CELEBRITIES

sneak through our cities in 30-foot limos

with tinted windows   eluding the riot of jealous eyes

they fancy in their guilt   and so make real

sniffing coke from silver platters and groping their plastic girls

behind the dark glass

as outside men with the faces of lions

grasp bottles in paper sacks and laugh up blood in alleyways

and women like wolves beckon lewdly with fingers like hooks

spitting out worms and rats

the celebrities crane their necks

to catch all the weird scenes on the street

but they can't get out

the natives would tear them to shreds

and the way inside is very tight

so it works out nearly even

WAY DOWN

in this town where

dim lights swing in mean homes

and cool eyes pop out any living room

just clicking from side to side

taking it all in sleepy and cool

kazoo-shaped eyes

there are clowns down here.

big smeared red grimace lips on a break from foolery

smoking fat brown cigars and growling dirty jokes

with their sleeves rolled up

underneath a bridge

saying "fuck" and "shit"

but still with some part of their hearts

that sets them apart from other men

and makes them clowns ha ha

    every night they lie back on their

misshapen cots, folding powerful arms behind their heads

    and sing themselves to sleep

sweet quiet phrases in deep drunk voices

.   "How beautiful you are,

how beautiful you are . . ."

Spaghetti and opera in their eyes.

SHADOW VALLEY

walking home tonight it's like writing a

long letter about going home

to the moon

tattooing it into the earth with my feet

for the moon to look down at and read

outside tonight in Denver a family of Quiet Things

is spitting silence all over the streets

I am a baby of blazing light

and I wander down here in the darkness

I put my lips to the bottle

and the bottle spreads its wings

and we fly down the valley together in love

CRAZY JOHNNY YUMA

the black sky spiky with peering stars

the spear-eyed sneering in velveteen bars

smearing bottles with their lips and

warming their hands at the fire

here in my head is the jewel called Look At The Goddess

here in my heart is the jewel called Serve The Queen

you'll see my face in the pool-table grinning felt-green   palpitating

my suit   which is a double-breasted wall of light

borrowed from the gods

I offer you this   as the thief

who has stolen it back for a second

MY POLITICS

I'm stunned and hurt, and I want to be free. I have heard of the horrible killings and deeds of cruelty and madness. I have heard about the wonderful light that melts and sweetens everything cold and hard, and heals the sick, and wakes the dead, and sends them stumbling back into the streets for more. My heart pounds. The stars wear cowboy boots.

The ghosts are misunderstood guests.

LISTEN

The messenger is under pressure. The future is after us.

ALBUQUERQUE

cool winds licked the streets

and made dead leaves sizzle

in driveways

I remember that sound

daddy daylight was down

mother sun was out

it was dark out there

and I heard the leaves rushing around

in the street outside

STATIC

His girl stood a few feet away with her hand on her mouth

amazed and a little embarrassed, I guess. She had short red hair
and a bright yellow dress on, a dragon tattooed on the

back of her leg. Maybe it was their first date and he hadn't

said anything to prepare her for this.

"It looks like a seizure," said Devin. "Do you know what to do?"

I didn't really but I'd been there before myself

and one hand washes the other so I waded over to him through
the static that had suddenly collected, and knelt there, cupping his
head

the kid shook

jackhammer-hard, bent upward strangely, throbbing,

lost, bell-bottoms trailing in his own spilled coffee, and I thought:
So that's how it looks from the outside.

"We just gotta hold his head up..." I narrated

"and don't put anything in his mouth . . ."

"Yeah," a voice spoke up from the crowd, "just hold him

so he knows someone's there."

And I'm willing to bet that kid

didn't know anybody was there, his jogging-shoes kicking in slow
mindless circles, but this guy seemed better-qualified, racing up

suddenly burly and very take-charge in a white sport-shirt, so I handed him over the kid's electrified head and backed off, feeling foolish and not very helpful.

At the counter it was business as usual

the register beeping and scooping in handfuls of jingling change

I stood there waiting for my refill and thought about death

all the doctors who told me: "A seizure can kill you"

the ER-tech who said, "It's like dying for a few minutes

each time you have one."

A guy in line before me jerked a thumb at the back of the room

where all the action was—"Too much espresso?" and grinned.

Well, that's the main sweetness of people, I guess, we go on

In circles, laughing at death, we take it in stride like the slow suicides we all are. Until it becomes a race, then sometimes we even win that for a long time before we finally lose it.

so "Yeah, ha-ha," I told the guy

More and more lately around here it seems like

the only people who raise much stink about

having to die anymore are the ones who

dislike being alive in the first place

and that philosophy kills.

I went back to the table with a new cup of coffee and

Devin was still sitting there. Some medics had shown up, they crouched in a circle around the kid, now sitting up and speaking thickly.

"You're coming out of it," they told him.

They asked him who the president was, what year it was

(I always used to hate that, especially during election years, when there were so many possibilities) then led him out to the waiting machine and loaded him in.

I glanced at the redhead. She smiled and gave a theatrical simper, embarrassed mostly. She kept looking at me. I looked away. Somebody came back with a mop and

cleaned up the spilled coffee

pushed the tables back together

where he'd fallen.

SHARP AND SWEET

Gangs push and pull on the hill.

Nightclubs open their tallowy legs

to receive all the creeps out there lonely.

Every thought is as real as a rock.

The pain comes and goes

like a thing breathing in and out.

No one is being betrayed.

This is the deal we made.

The basket of water breaks in your womb

and a wrinkled head forces its way out yelling.

Outside cops in flying saucers comb the parking lot

with waves of light.

RTD JOURNALS #7

I stood at the bus-stop in my paper-thin gray jacket staring down at the dingy sidewalk as cars and noises and pieces of trash blew past.

There were a lot of street-people at the bus-stop, and more were approaching in single file from the temp labor place on High St. They all had puffy orange and blue BRONCOS jackets to keep them warm.

I stood there shivering, thinking about my life.

A woman in a kerchief I'd seen out there the day before flagging down cars, tall and thin, with a long thin snakelike neck, approached me with a palm full of bus-

tokens: "Hey bayby, wanna buy some tokens?"

"I have a student pass."

"*Aw* yeah." She knew about the student pass

A burly green mound of a man with an oxygen tank and plastic nose plugs struggled rapidly over the street through the cars and noises and pieces of trash that kept coming and coming in the cold wind, and sat down hard on the bench. The woman hailed him—"Wussup!"—and walked over swinging her arms.

"Ain't seen you in a long time . . . what you been up to?"

"Thinkin' 'bout *you!*"

His voice was rough and thick, inhuman, altered, the

voice of an ape or a bear

"Well, you better cut that out," she said warningly

"Yeah, I don' have any money!" he quipped

She laughed and said, "So what you been up to?"

"I had a heart attack last week!"

"You had a heart-attack last week an' you out here smokin'?"

"Yes ma'am! I'm ready to go with my mama an' daddy!"

The woman laughed again as though here, indeed,

was something truly delicious, then asked, "So where they at,

up in Arkansas somewhere?"

"Naw . . ."

"Where they at?"

"Heaven!" he roared in a ragged dark-brown bass, and patted the oxygen tank

with real warmth

"Oh, you mean you ready to die?"

"Yeah . . ."

She walked away quickly, looking bored. I looked over at the guy with the oxygen tank, he looked warm sitting there in his green ski-jacket, all bundled up there on the bench getting ready for death

The bus came and only a few of us actually boarded.

Rolling down Colfax toward Downing, the driver said, "Downing!" then gave an eerie screaming cackle that lasted all the way to the stop

We all wondered about it, I guess

REMEMBER

I want you to bring in the sculpture near the beginning of the

show and activate it.

PLANET LADY

I will lay down the vows I have made. I will make new vows.

Join me in the rows of corn, I will make a ceremony

out of pebbles and stones and launch my heart my

way of milking light. I will get on my knees.

Cut to ribbons by light

In the moment of lions

of Saturday night, cast ashore

like a shipwreck, moored

in the deepest fibers like a

stubborn stain. I will always

come back to you, in the rocks

like mirrors, the roots and nerves

branching and spawning below

the soil. In the cool, oil-filled

glow of the gas-station,

closer to you.

THOUSANDS OF YEARS

My cat is asleep on the bed with slits for eyes

    dreaming of things that dart away.

Cars are lowing like cows in the street outside

and ruined men with rotting noses

are rooting through trash for scraps of meat

in the alley behind my house.

The occasional single gunshot in the distance is heard

when somebody gives up

and the sidewalk just lying there

night after night accepting all the spots and stains and

nameless chunks without complaint.

Oceans away all the mummies of Underground Egypt

sleep swaddled in gauze down deep airless shafts

waiting thousands of years

to become butterflies

or the Judgment of Man

and this sweet little animal

is safe at home on Earth.

CHILDHOOD

A little boy who received a book that brought stars and angels clanging against his windowsill . . . who saw gangsters and bums in the clouds . . . sold his soul for a knife on the threepenny streets . . . explosive things and lit things . . . firecrackers and bombs . . .

Most people just don't notice.

The war goes on around them.

He peeled the plastic strips with his name and address off the sides

of the box and pasted them inside above the pizza before eating any. The next morning he looked out the window and downstairs in the courtyard, growing out of an arrangement of circular stones like a giant pepperoni pizza in the snow was an old brown tree standing vigil like a cross.

THE TOTAL WORK OF ART

The drugs are inside me   glass cities as far as the eye can see
The seahorses are up in the rafters   a whole family of them is up
there

Most of the time   my heart seems to know where it's going

it yanks me along   but my heart can be wrong

At least we could sit there drinking together like fish

stuffing four-legged creatures into our mouths   in the next few
days   if we concentrate

I'm as drunk as a fish

I will work you with all of my heart

WHERE GREASY DUCKTAILS ARE

SMOOTHED INTO PLACE

at stoplights and drunk Indians lie in the road with their feet cut off. "They cut my feet off," says the guy, and I believe him. Then he walks over and gets in the road and lies down. The road stinks with an eerie dim green in broad daylight. The trash keeps coming and coming in the cold wind and piling wherever it stops. There are piles and piles of bottles and cigarette-butts and used condoms, newspapers and wrappers and liners at every curbstone, at the foot of each wall. The whole place stinks of giving-up.

This is where Spider-man goes when he wants information about the Green Goblin. A bar with glowing bottles at the end of the night where the whole neighborhood gets baby-eyed. A crowded room of cocky, sullen teens and grizzled bastards washed up from the motorcycle street.

My veins are the streets of this city, my body. Skid row is my stomach.

A river of bile flows past the brass rail, the

air buckles with jazz, a cork pops,

a green spray of bright notes dances

out of the jukebox,

FIRE DINER

the door

slams, a pin drops,

a dog barks, a glass breaks,

      and day by day

   us green-faced fools who live by the river

   all fold our plantlike hands and

      pray pray pray in the usual way

THE SNAKE OIL ADDICT

I don't want excellence anymore.

Just getting by is enough to thrill me blind.

My language is sticky and tragic with

image and magic just talking about a

dishwashing detergent or some new

remote-control gadget.

Maybe everyone suffers exactly

the same amount.

Bankers and lawyers

and starving children

and people in wheelchairs

whether or not they race

or play basketball in them.

All the celebrities,

FIRE DINER

Jesus H. Christ

and the garbage-men

and me.

We all weather the same unending assault. We all know death

is the only unbeatable game, we all know that's our name.

We just mark it with different words and ways of knowing

because we're vain.

Cause we don't know what to do

or where to go to kill the pain:

a bar? a church? the bus-station?

a vial of pills? an airplane?

Everyone wants to be brave and

unique and right but it only happens sometimes

And so maybe we'll never quite know anybody,

just the outlines and reflections

of ourselves

and maybe it's better that way.

I'm content with the kind of excellence prized among

used-car dealers, that dubious excellence won by

certain brands of soap and toilet-paper. The truly

excellent things would blow my mind, would be too

huge and fierce for me to cognize

at this stage of my decline.

In my city, if you want, for the next few days,

if there's someone you really hate, you can hire

one of "Santa's helpers" to deliver a sock-full of

chunks of coal direct to that person's door on

Xmas morning for 20 bucks. I saw the ad.

But talking to the people we love is very difficult.

Even the people we like.

Below that was the number to call for Denver's

Hottest Singles. I thought about calling, but I have enough

trouble with women as it is.

Below that was GET RICH STUFFING ENVELOPES FOR

CASH,and below that was SMOKE POT, GET PAID.

I wrote the numbers down.

Perfection is just the way I like my

cheese melted at TACO BELL,

melted

to perfection

AND THE YELLOW LAND YAWNED

A red-and-white Ford Fairlane from the golden age of

rock and roll was paused outside the pale-blue

breakfast-joint with its top down, sharp and sleek like a

cigarette-boat, channeled and chopped to catch the glare and

throw it back pink.

Getting out of the truck Lee Ann said, "That's the car I want

someday, a Fairlane . . . mmm . . ."

smiling her mystery smile in a language that

bats speak, of outlines, reflections of sounds, and

shifting her Oriental almost Egyptian eyes at me

disarmingly slightly, "only mine will be blue, like a

powder-blue, you know?"

"Yeah," I said.

A woman of late-middle-age sat, legs crossed, in the cafe corner, abbreviated beehive frosted pale-blonde and pinned to her head with pearl earrings—a real Dale-Evans-type—kicking her ankles in red high-heels and making small-talk with the man at the nearest table.

FIRE DINER

"I bet she owns the Fairlane," said Lee Ann.

"I bet so too," I said, "she looks like class."

The breakfast came.

Driving away down a long straight road between two

flat fields, she said, "Steer for a second, will you?"

then she bent down to reset the player.

I took the wheel and looked out the windshield.

The sky was clear and blue and cold and bright and quiet and wide. The sun was shining. The air was sweet. Then she came up smiling and took back the wheel. I leaned over and kissed her on the ivory nape, then sat back very straightly against the seat, my nose full of colorful smells of her soft dark hair, her cool pale skin.

It's like drowning

or falling asleep

or fighting a blackout in public:

your head keeps diving at the floor,

and your mind keeps pulling it back.

Our speech is so dreamlike sometimes, I think back later

and can't tell whether I've dreamed it or not—like the time I said I used to have a goatee, and she said, "You're a goat!"

and I said, "You're a *boat*!"

—did that really happen?

I leaned over and kissed her again and our glasses clicked

and I said, "I'll buy you a car like that someday."

"Okay. Make it a blue one."

Bumping along the brown road, her pearly presence at my side
and her hand on my knee with pink glow-in-the-dark nail-polish
feeding a warm strong pulse all the way up my thigh to my heart—
bolts of hay at the edge of the red field, the brown road shaking
beneath us, the cold sun smiling, the yellow land yawning . . .

I'll never give my heart away so foolishly again.
They'll have to come and get it next time.

GENERATION X THINKS ABOUT SOAP OPERAS

Doctor Cham-Pog became a nanny when his wife died. He was later found guilty of holding seven dead people hostage, along with his mother, who then died, and he killed himself. His daughter, GOGDA CHAG-MOP, married a dead cow when she was twelve, using the stiffened udders as phalluses. She later killed all their children in BIZARRE RIRUAL SEX ORGY BLOODBATH, was found smoking pot near her mother's house, who had just died. Soon Bilbo Cham-Pot became heroin addict, killed ten newborn babies smashed eggshell head bloody again and again, and hanged himself. His son, KOG BOGCHAR, killed everyone else except Nancy. Very soon Nancy POTONG became TWA pilot crashed into hillside killing thousands of people, was later found gibbering and moaning in the cellar with a man in a rubber clown suit, dead. Tune in Tuesdays at 8 for more thrilling episodes!

THE DEVIL'S BARN

Everybody felt like that

we wanted to throw

the radio out the window

Doom tasted like Joy

The stars hung in the

sky like fish-hooks

We felt like that

All matter was moving

All matter was

met

and

bent

and melted

by Mind

some golden doors worth

$10,000 were melted

FIRE DINER

and rivers of gold

ran into the sewer

The Mayor got pretty

upset but

thanks to God and the ATF

no celebrities were

seriously burned

(after a while it got so bad

I couldn't even sit down

for fear all the chairs had

"power")

POTS AND PANS

The night is cold and flesh is sold   in galleries just down the road

Long spaces of silence are speech   and the stars are knives

that stab at your eyes

You stumble home past churches and brick shit-houses

all the pots and pans hating the buildings they live in

All the houses are heads   and the windows are eyes

each house has a different haircut

At home,

this is goddam

serious business, lazy

electric red lilies asleep in the window, your eyes

playing tennis with stars and light

in a glass frying pan

all night

and sometimes you think you can get it

and you stick out your tongue for the pearl

and sometimes you see it   and sometimes you get it

and sometimes you never get it

Sometimes you just keep asking

SOMETIMES IT'S A JOYRIDE, EXHAUST PIPES FLASHING IN THE SUNSET ZOOM

You get there. You have dreams. You love someone.

The only certainty infection with illusion. Some people are there. You try to make plans. It breaks down. You keep going. It hurts. There are books to read, statues to look at. It breaks down again. You keep going. You're the only one there. You're the only thing real.

How he sees the world. It happens all at once.

The bloody mess under the sheet behind a wall of riot shields.

A storm of light on the plane of time.

The eyes you screw into your face every morning.

THE WATER PARTY

They threw frogs into the sea.

They threw birds at the sun.

I was drunk when I got there,

and started out with water.

All the bugs and spiders were stuffed back into their nests

and the holes were plugged.

Kristi knocked over my water and brought me back a vodka-tonic.

Jamie showed up in a checked sport coat and at first I didn't recognize him. All the trees released their grip and toppled to earth like an army enchanted to sleep. The sun gobbled the clouds.

The seas were drained, their finny dead plowed under.

All the mountains slumped over like drunks into powdery heaps and It got very quiet.

Some kids from D.U. showed up and smoked hash with us,

braying like donkeys and calling each other "bro."

All the people were taken away in a truck and burned

for hygienic reasons.

My eyes developed a painful film.

I reached into my drink and rubbed an ice cube over the lids.

It felt good, like getting brand-new eyes.

The few surviving animals made their way to the dry ocean-beds
where they lived for a while on seaweed and the like

but not long without water. It seemed endless to them

and their anguished bawling filled the air.

 I looked up from my burger and Jessica gave me a funny smile
that lingered slightly. It cheered me.

"Y'onna diet?" quipped the waiter

when Paul said all he wanted was water.

My arm slid off the table and my

right eye rolled to follow it.

Finally they turned off the sun and it was possible to sleep.

IN TEXAS

The mud in the alleys was yellow and rich, like rivers of fecal honey. Huge clattering beetles flew into our faces. She seemed so exotic to me. A ring in her nose and her hair tied up in green locks, a red western-style leather jacket with studs, and a padlocked collar around her neck.

And she seemed so exotic her pale sharp features and

soft, spiky, dinosaur-backed Texas accent.

We sat down in somebody's driveway to watch the sunset.

The rain had stopped   the crickets were loud. Katherine read me her story of a boy named Henry who lived on Presidents' Island, a toxic-waste dump near Galveston. I thought it was good. It really flew. Then she gave me my first taste of hot pickled okra. A combination of spines and honey.

When it had no form.

When it came from Heaven raw.

THE THIEF

I want to make romantic gestures

go out of my way at great length

the blade of your neck

the wings of your elbows

you haunt the inside of my mask with wanting

and glasses of wine that sing

I've seen you before

your luminous accent

the wings and blades of your hollow bones

your eyes hair smell

imagining

the warm feeling I get

when your blue eyes go over me

stupider and stupider with roses

this kid has no limit

the thief has moved through

all the rooms in this house

like a broom

WILLPOWER

He was in white robes   he thought it was ABOUT TO CHANGE

He asked them if they thought it was ABOUT TO CHANGE

the others gathered around him there

and they said they thought it was ABOUT TO HAPPEN

and hell, sure, yes

there were bound to be changes

He stayed home smoking pot all day

watching talk-shows on TV

only stirred from his lair in the late afternoon to pace the streets
cars shooting past   joggers prancing around him

worried about how fast he was going

There came a terrible beautiful moment one night when he
thought: Holy shit, I've done it. I've lost my fucking mind. I'm crazy
now and I can't change back. I have to live this way. He thought:
FUCK . . .Fuck.

He stood on the sidewalk outside the beer store, all the cars shooting past, hundreds thousands of people in Denver all pressed in tightly together like bees like ants, alive and sweating, hating it, fighting it.

He went inside and bought a six-pack then he came back out, a smile on his face, his breath ragged and quick. All these years of letting himself lose more and more of his mind on purpose, to see if there might be something underneath, and more and more, there wasn't.

FAME

I'm talking about the Juggernaut

UNDERNEATH my mind. You people

shoulda stayed outta the studio,

this is a radio program, this is

a radio program, this is a radio

program. This is not a recording.

What are you teaching these

children? This is sick! This is

a radio broadcast: Neptune

and his Chlorine Children.

Piss and demons.

Go down into the city

and see how it feels in the city

on Christmas Eve

be a pale thinking force in the city

find a way to explode the narrative

without saying that.

We all have a dopey, gregarious

"Uncle Charlie"

we'd like to see in show business

but now is not the time.

FROM A SPEEDING CAR

The trees on a hill

burning chemical flame

in lime-green

fiery orange

and red

and blue-pink

sending colorful

chemical

hormones

out from the cores of

their long straight trunks

to the tips of the

thousands of leaves that

hover around them on stalks.

The trees are tall

and stand thin watching

The highway muscles

through below, the metal

boxes speeding along

hard

against the rusty

guard-rail

and cruising along

as fast as they can

in their rush to

destroy everything

the trees are watching you

THE SUN

It looked like you were

trying to capture lightning.

We rode motorcycles

over the hills

to the junkheap

all the mangled, twisted

wreckage, and there

we saw the Sun.

I'm here in your town and I'm worth just as much

as the Sun! shouted angry young men who

had had enough of the Sun. I've been looking at you, your

wild eyes. You didn't know I was a devil at first. That's just because

I'm a gentleman.

Me and you in the moon-yard.

The blue bar room.

The dancing blue motherfucking twisted blue

steel wreckage night. The molten

yearbook crown of thorns inter-

rupted passage alone alone

and haunted empty hungry lonely

night.

It

never

felt

so

good.

WESTERNERS

this time of year

I wonder what it is

I feel all the dead leaves under my shoes

the giant cold weather outside makes you feel very small and

warm in here, and all your

fears and plans of the outside world look

vain and false   it's so much bigger than you

out there   that weather   so cold

so towering   tall   and vast

tomorrow I'll go for a walk

all the way to the bank

all the way to the store and back

all the way to the bookstore

the record store

K-Mart

The Tattered Cover

Fahrenheit's

Safeway   all the way to the barbershop and back

with snow on the ground

dead leaves under my shoes

the ground under my shoes

televisions dictating

a muttering sadness behind every wall

with the sun in the sky staring at me

tomorrow

behind a thin layer of clouds

A MORNING SHOW BANNED IN THE WEST AND
MADE INTO A LATE-LATE

Where the taxi-driver makes no sense,

his speech a silent bloom of light and bubbles, how fish speak.

He asks for directions and mumbles a drunken kerplunk as he plops into traffic.

Where things take place underwater. Where nurses rub alcohol into your wounds. Out here on the edge of the city where bums heat dimes with their hands and gangs of wild children talk sex in the shadows. Late-night porn in the motel room and shivering corn in my head, the void. As a private detective I will have to consider you all suspects.

I was there and I saw what happened. I saw you dancing with fire in your mouth among them. With one of them putting its arms around you. Where angels hallow the huddled child, and old men climb to the stars in rocking chairs. Where buses nose down tilted streets making gasping stops and thieves get high on dark rooftops and hidden clowns in strange positions smile. I can love you and get lost down in the black hole of you but you will always be a suspect.

Your face came apart in my hands like gingerbread. You lost your shape. The New Thing came forward to stare at the world, eyes blinked, and altars bled. Your teeth melting, your eyes pinwheeling, your breath rushing out in diamonds of pearls of hot breath

your whole slippery body was full of hot stars.

Even those of us who worship light were blinded.

Rock and roll and life and going on put their arms around you

and helped you stumble home just in time for the creepshow.

When doves were bombs from Heaven. When LSD was the spider-spangled Truth. When dead girls led us home through the swamp and we held their pale hands and thought the world had really ended. Damp voices told a dark opera, and greenery shook. Something snagged under the wheels and we both thought we heard a faint cry but we didn't say anything. Hearts get numb in the city.

THE SECRET AGENTS

Kerosene breath in the radiator,

evil hitch-hikers with knives in their boots coming

out of the abandoned gas station and fanning out

across the black hill studded with crosses from old gunfights

like crows rushing along a fence.

The secret agents laid down a path through the treetops. Birds squawked. Pint-sized secret agents slipping through the keyhole with parachutes. Beautiful worlds exploded in the ends of their cigarettes, expanded into the twilight as smoke, the gorgeous lit thought set afire, and passing trains cast rays that went all different ways over all the rooftops and numbered plastic surfaces of the dark dirty city. Way back at the dawn of time before we existed where crows dance in the sunspots.

DAYLIGHT

that brightly wiggling enemy

of whom we all know, and cocks crow . . .

bums on the sidewalk with black eyes asking for change

like the Zombies of Money

angels with black lips

sneering from nightclub doorways

groggy, drunk, lost in the sunshine,

squinting like cats and

stretching their spines against

storefronts

. . . our puny two-legged doings here below.

Daylight, you omnivorous flame,

you maniac advancing from the shadows with your club

how far into me you see.

UNFORGOTTEN

My father died tonight.

I walked in and he died right away. His mouth was open.

Lightning struck outside and shook the shadows around the window. It was dark.

Some others were there. My mother was there, and my sister.

Some people from the church. I got there right on time.

It rained a few minutes.

The body just lay there with its mouth open, dead,

huge impossible presence in the room.

That shock rang in me, but I didn't say much. It wasn't real.

I said "Thank you" into his ear and kissed him on the forehead when I left.

THE SMELL OF LIMES

The heart is a huge and silent matter.

This is what we have waited for   to understand

the unspeakable

The gods have always lived underground   deep inside us

Your lover has been dancing in your arms the whole time

Neptune and Pluto are there in your neurons   weightless

Your lover is a fluttering spirit with butterfly wings who will

never never leave you

On this beautiful night   we eat fruit from the planet

We stand under the fountain with gushing hearts

like fish pulled out of the ocean

with darting eyes

going into white light

and even tiny particles love you

When every little atom is awake

PURGATORY

Giddy celebration in the face of doom

Is more heroic than martyrdom . . .

throwing berries in the jaws of death.

But all heroism is martyrdom,

whether or not the hero's drunk.

Think of your heroes.

    So I don't want to be a hero . . .

I just wanna be drunk when doom hits me

I want someone's arms to be around me

when the wind blows down this town

when ghosts rustle on the mesa . . .

there may or may not be heroes

anywhere

anymore

ever

after this

    . . . so don't come unglued.

THE PULL OF THE DROP

Stepping carefully through

the exquisite hell prepared for me

   and my feet are large and strong

the soles are hard like hammered copper

I could walk a long way   miles

   from a hell of burning   to a hell of drowning   then the next

      thing you know

it's a hell of shrinking   or a hell of floating   a hell of flashing lights

   or biting flies   it could take years

but I'm already here

   with a basket of light   on your doorstep

You can eat my heart if you want   it's made of meat

   you can swallow my soul if you're hungry

      I have miles of untapped soul   I ought to drill a well

So let the people gather in the fields as they may

FIRE DINER

and marvel at the patterns in the sky

    some stupid stargazers thought up   but it's true

If you have to split I'll pay for the cab

if you want to eat shit then split

go ahead it's OK   I'll pay

I'll cut off my feet and

hang them around my neck

on a silver chain

    whatever you say

THE STUPID LONESOME

voodoo doll

crawled up the hillside on his

hands and knees through a

hollow log and over

and under some

barbed-wire fences through

a smell of campfires and

meat cooking and

threw himself down

on his back at the

top of the hill

slowly pulled the pins out

of his eyes and

marveled at the patterns

some stupid stargazers

thought up

MODERN ART

All your cultural heroes

you thought were such rebels

turn out to be deep cover agents

and what you admire was

a government plot all along.

The orderly ranks of bottles

behind the bar reflecting light

mock the spinning-eyed drunkard

who can barely keep his shoulders

together, who can barely keep

from splitting in two charred

halves right there

split open by lightning

at the bar

Pigs turn into spiders.

Children into murderers.

Nothingness is pumped into the grass,

and the hot air flickers, receiving it.

My spider sense is tingling.

The children have descended into the subway,

Where flesh eaters prowl, and leviathans flail.

The constant static is flowing power noise, is

God's Broadcast to them, elemental children

with teeth like knives

in the belly of the subway

on zero gravity pills.

IN KANSAS

We got stuck in the full moon

coming back from the liquor store   our

mouths full of mushy fruit

some girl gave us

at the After Dark Trailer Park

eyes like brake-lights

eyes like the red lights

that blink on the radio towers

around here that water our town with

Classic Rock and commercials for trucks

and puffy treats

COUNTRY LIVING

After Death, the part of God you're in, the part of your Soul you believed was underwater, comes above ground, and the dry part, the conscious you, drowns. All this is precisely arranged in a marketplace. The dogs follow strangers. You go drown in the worm eaten night. The coffee house has glowing light you hide in, outside the blizzard, the asking for more, saying, "please." For just a cup of soup or a thin thread of heated liquid. Something brittle in a kimono romanced in the cab of a pickup truck then tossed away like wadded condoms or a tuft of cigarette smoke at the drive in movies all night long in Bedside Manner, Texas, where the pitchforks kiss the haystacks and the tombstones suck the sky. And farmers produced milk and eggs. Formed everything into a neat cardboard package. Powdered milk was condensed in aluminum cans wrapped tightly in cellophane. And the midnight-men tore apart cars, but no one talked about it, ever. And the bullies played baseball, grateful for the dirty roots of everything. And heat whispered in the pipes of the hospital. And the secret agents found their way in through the cracks in the side of the trailer where the toilet was, and rappelled, using dental floss, down to the tortured floorboards at the bottom of the cabinet.

"NOW LET'S HAVE A PICNIC!"

I remember a moment

of looking at you

something true in your face

that was talking to me

it was gum on the tip of my mind

it was sugar and glue on my tongue   all week long

I was looking at you

every inch of the skin on your face told me feelings

the conversation was a gooey blob

we bounced between us wordless

now and then   somehow I think we told each other something

all week long   and I wonder what you thought

it was very impressive

most of all

I remember the moon

peeking out from the clouds

then concealing itself

as the clouds shook and turned

then popping back out from another

pale shelf of blue clouds drowning deep

in the dark blue sky

the moon playing hopscotch for us

the good sweet moon

I remember you told me, "it's full,"

and it was

ARMCHAIR FRANKENSTEINS

The problems of a scientist. Travel. Trouble.

Chaos slips out from under the analytic bludgeon.

The present is a purifying hell. The force I ride is the future.

I didn't go out with you into the drunken black night because I didn't want my neck broke under the black stars. I like mellow scenes.

The gentlemen are waiting in the churchyard with the tools. There's a jug stashed under the wagon. These gentlemen drink strange liquids under the stars.

The night is shining like a silver tooth. The fog is on display.

There may be some kind of patrol so keep down and radio in if you have any travel. Trouble. You and the force you rode in on.

The monster is underneath a blanket in the back of the wagon. There may be some kind of alarm. I'm standing in the church and I can already smell the fumes.

All the houses have haircuts and eyes.

Every house has a different haircut.

And you kneel at the banks of the deep river sifting the

powdered smashed buildings for saleable baubles

unharmed in the blast.

All over the city, it's Sunday morning.

Get in there, you garbage-handlers!

THE SARCASTIC INDIAN

On the day of a million enemies

old mister respect took his hammock

down beside the river and strung it

between two trees.

He was fast asleep when

enemies took all his weapons.

Enemies hid his tomahawk

inside a haystack

on the day of a million deadly enemies

and they carried his haircut away in a sack

old mister garbage,

old mister bottomless-wells.

Years later his fire-breathing grandson

worked at the gas-station.

RTD JOURNALS # 17

A guy spoke up from the seat behind me. "You are all . . . crim-CHA!" A little old man near the front door turned around for a second, then back again, staring out the window of the bus. I didn't turn around.

The voice went on. "Crim-CHA . . . does not know he is *crim*-cha, but he is *CRIM*-cha . . . criminals . . . you are all criminals . . . crim-CHA does not like crim-CHA . . . crim-CHA will do anything to *destroy* crim-CHA . . . You do not believe you are crim-CHA but one day what I say . . . shall become law . . . you will all be called . . . crim-CHA . . . criminals . . ."

I kept wanting to turn around, even ask the guy a question, but I didn't. Finally he got off the bus at 3rd and Broadway and I caught a glimpse as he went down the back stairs. His skin was brown and his eyes were slanted. The tops of his ears were covered by his hat.

Everything was so much more important than I'd ever realized. I became convinced there was a far smaller amount of time left than anyone seemed to believe. This is emergency surgery in the back of a truck with a Swiss army knife.

THE WONDERFUL JACKET

The rays coming from the people

in this room. This precise evening,

when it is necessary to strike.

Bob and Jean Moth-Heart will be there at the head of the parade.

They have a house and a car and a crewcut lawn and an
answering machine that goes: "Hi, you've reached Bob and Jean
Moth-Heart!"

Now that we have arranged a committee.

Listen to me I sweat and

have a body and shit and

cry like you.

I want to tell you about my romantic bohemian lifestyle in Flesh
Demon City

Every darkened doorway holds a killer with a dagger

FIRE DINER

Every night a great drunk artist splashing blackness everywhere

The streets will be clogged with

people. The only mammals able

to get a suntan are pigs and

people. Animals. Mammals.

This sunburn will teach you to behave

with good morals and common sense.

This toothpaste will restore your

conscience.

OUTSIDER ART

When I'm telling the truth, people think I'm joking

When I'm joking, they think I'm crazy, or drunk

When I'm drunk, they think I'm drunk

it's a delicate balance

           (but I'm rarely drunk)

They think I think whatever they think I think

and they're usually wrong

so if you don't think it's funny

I can say, "Well goddam, I was telling

The TRUTH, don't be CRUEL!"

           (to a heart that's true) ♫

and if you don't like what I think,

I can say "Lighten UP,

I'm only KIDDING!"

It gives me a back door of sorts.

FIRE DINER

I'd rather be crazy than sane anyway

Most of you people seem

so very sad and small-hearted

you dumb proud angels, you idiot stars

but all the mistakes are worthwhile

    I love being misunderstood by you all, it's an honor

Whatever it is you think I think

    I'm glad you're not ignoring me

MEANING

They were all scared of life

so they worshipped death,

built temples to death,

drove cars of death,

went to work and

sweated at thankless

jobs of death

in factories of death,

had nervous breakdowns

from the stress

and were

institutionalized

in hospitals of death

and paid for it all with

money of death

and

somewhere

deep in Maple Moses,

a little pig was

flying around a little tree

probably.

www.ingramcontent.com/pod-product-compliance
Lightning Source LLC
Chambersburg PA
CBHW071826020426
42331CB00007B/1617